Awake
in the
Wild

Awake
in the
Wild

Reconnect With Nature and Discover Yourself

Illustrations by
Madalina Andronic

Quarto is the authority on a wide range of topics.

Quarto educates, entertains and enriches the lives of our readers—enthusiasts and lovers of hands-on living.

www.quartoknows.com

First published in the United States of America in 2017 by
Rock Point Gift and Stationery, a member of
Quarto Publishing Group USA Inc.
142 West 36th Street, 4th Floor
New York, New York 10018
www.quartoknows.com

10 9 8 7 6 5 4 3 2 1

Designed by Jen Cogliantry

ISBN 978-1-63106-298-8

Printed in China

Contents

Introduction

> "A morning glory at the window satisfies me more than
> the metaphysics of books."
>
> —Walt Whitman

Observation is its own form of meditation and, like meditation, it is a skill that will enrich your life in a multitude of ways if you nurture it and allow it to flourish. It entails slowing down enough to really see what it is you are looking at. The difference between looking and seeing may at first seem impossibly subtle, but with further exploration you will discover what a profound difference it is. Imagine stopping to smell the roses, but as you are deeply inhaling their sweet perfume you also notice the sturdy pride of each stem, the scalloped edges of the leaves, the rich color of the flower, and the tiny insect dancing across the velvety curve of the petals. With a bit of practice, observing things will become second nature and you will gain a deeper understanding of the natural world around you and, in turn, yourself.

How To Use This Journal

Nature is everywhere you live, whether in the city or the country. What plants and trees and birds and insects do you see on your way to work? Is there a flower growing in the crack of a sidewalk? Can you hear birds singing in the morning or squirrels chattering? Concentrate on hearing the subtle layer of sound under the sounds that dominate your environment.

Notice the feel of sunshine or the breeze on your skin. Do you smell cut grass? At first you may not see or hear or feel much, but the more you pay attention the more you will notice.

Take time out of your day, or plan on weekends, to focus your attention on the natural environment. Tune in and observe the nature you encounter every day.

Here's a simple exercise. Think of that tree you walk past all the time. Look carefully and make a point of noticing something new about it each day. Touch the bark and note its texture. See the veins in the leaves when the sun filters through them. Notice new growth, like buds on branches. Are there flowers? Is there a nest somewhere on a branch above? Are there insects on the trunk?

Now turn that same focus towards your own moods, thoughts, and feelings. and jot down your observations—what you saw in nature, when you saw it, how it made you feel, and, perhaps, how it relates to your own life and its cycles. Year after year, over the next five years, write down your observations and reflect on your previous writings.

Be sure to read over your earlier journal entries as the years pass. Work on focusing and expanding the details of your observations. Detail what you have seen, where you have visited, and how you felt during these times. Your journaling will improve, your concentration skills will be honed, and you will become a true "seer" of nature.

"Nature" is What We See
by Emily Dickinson

"Nature" is what we see—
The Hill—the Afternoon—
Squirrel—Eclipse—the Bumble bee—
Nay—Nature is Heaven—
Nature is what we hear—
The Bobolink—the Sea—
Thunder—the Cricket—
Nay—Nature is Harmony—
Nature is what we know—
Yet have no art to say—
So impotent Our Wisdom is
To her Simplicity.

How to Meditate

Meditation can help you become a better observer of our natural world. Set aside a dedicated time every day—all you need is five minutes to start. The real goal is to be as consistent as possible so that it becomes a ritual. Mornings are an ideal time to meditate, before things become hectic and the day gets away from you. Try to slip it into your schedule right after you wake up. Starting and sticking to a meditation routine can be as simple as setting your alarm ten minutes earlier than usual.

Sit up comfortably and close your eyes. Concentrate on your breathing. Take deep inhales and exhales. Fill your up lungs each time you breathe in, empty them completely each time you breathe out. Feel your chest rise and fall, listen to the sound of each breath as it enters and leaves your body. Try inhaling to a slow count of four and exhaling to a slow count of four. The act of counting is soothing and will help keep other thoughts quiet.

Don't attempt to forcibly clear your mind, just focus on breathing and let your mind settle into a quiet space. If something distracts you— a noise, a smell, a thought—acknowledge it and then let it go. The key is to try and stay in the moment and not worry about what happened yesterday or what obligations lie throughout the day ahead. Staying present can be quite challenging. Whenever you notice your thoughts drifting, bring them back to your breath.

Don't beat yourself up if you find your mind wandering. The more you practice, the better you will become at letting things go and you may even find yourself being able to meditate for longer and longer periods of time. But no matter what, know that you are not doing it wrong. Give yourself permission to struggle. Be kind to yourself. Meditation is a gift you are giving to yourself, a gift you deserve, and simply making room for it in your life is a tremendous accomplishment. Well done!

"For seen with the eye of the poet,
as God sees them, all things are
alive and beautiful."
—Henry David Thoreau

The Art of Seeing Things

by John Burroughs, from *"Leaf and Tendril"*, 1908.

So far as seeing things is an art, it is the art of keeping your eyes and ears open. The art of nature is all in the direction of concealment. The birds, the animals, all the wild creatures, for the most part try to elude your observation. The art of the bird is to hide her nest; the art of the game you are searching for is to make itself invisible. The flower seeks to attract the bee and the moth by its color and perfume, because they are of service to it; but I presume it would hide from the excursionists and the picnickers if it could, because they extirpate it. Power of attention and a mind sensitive to outward objects, in these lies the secret of seeing things. Can you bring all your faculties to the front, like a house with many faces at the doors and windows; or do you live retired within yourself, shut up in your own meditations? The thinker puts all the powers of his mind in reflection: the observer puts all the powers of his mind in perception; every faculty is directed outward; the whole mind sees through the eye and hears through the ear. He has an objective turn of mind as opposed to a subjective. A person with the latter turn of mind sees little. If you are occupied with your own thoughts, you may go through a museum of curiosities and observe nothing.

Of course one's powers of observation may be cultivated as well as anything else. The senses of seeing and hearing may be quickened and trained as well as the sense of touch. Blind persons come to be marvelously acute in their powers of touch. Their feet find the path and keep it. They come to know the lay of the land through this sense, and recognize the roads and surfaces they have once traveled over. Helen Keller reads your speech by putting her hand upon your lips, and is thrilled by the music of an instrument through the same sense of touch. The perceptions of school-children should be trained as well as their powers of reflection and memory. A teacher in Connecticut, Miss Aiken,—whose work on mind-training I commend to all teachers,— has hit upon a simple and ingenious method of doing this. She has a revolving blackboard upon which she writes various figures, numbers, words, sentences, which she exposes to the view of the class for one or two or three seconds, as the case may be, and then asks them to copy or repeat what was written. In time they become astonishingly quick, especially the girls, and can take in a multitude of things at a glance. Detectives, I am told, are trained after a similar method; a man is led quickly by a show-window, for instance, and asked to name and describe the objects he saw there. Life itself is of course more or less a school of this kind, but the power of concentrated attention in most persons needs stimulating. Here comes in the benefit of manual-training schools. To *do* a thing, to make something, the powers of the mind must be focused. A boy in building a boat will get something that all the books in the world cannot give him. The concrete, the definite, the discipline of real things, the educational values that lie here, are not enough appreciated.

The book of nature is like a page written over or printed upon with different-sized characters and in many different languages, interlined and cross-lined, and with a great variety

of marginal notes and references. There is coarse print and fine print; there are obscure signs and hieroglyphics. We all read the large type more or less appreciatively, but only the students and lovers of nature read the fine lines and the footnotes. It is a book which he reads best who goes most slowly or even tarries long by the way. He who runs may read some things. We may take in the general features of sky, plain, and river from the express train, but only the pedestrian, the saunterer, with eyes in his head and love in his heart, turns every leaf and peruses every line. One man sees only the migrating water-fowls and the larger birds of the air; another sees the passing kinglets and hurrying warblers as well. For my part, my delight is to linger long over each page of this marvelous record, and to dwell fondly upon its most obscure text.

I take pleasure in noting the minute things about me. I am interested even in the ways of the wild bees, and in all the little dramas and tragedies that occur in field and wood. One June day, in my walk, as I crossed a rather dry, high-lying field, my attention was attracted by small mounds of fresh earth all over the ground, scarcely more than a handful in each. On looking closely, I saw that in the middle of each mound there was a hole not quite so large as a lead-pencil. Now, I had never observed these mounds before, and my curiosity was aroused. "Here is some fine print," I said, "that I have overlooked." So I set to work to try to read it; I waited for a sign of life. Presently I saw here and there a bee hovering about over the mounds. It looked like the honey-bee, only less pronounced in color and manner. One of them alighted on one of the mounds near me, and was about to disappear in the hole in the center when I caught it in my hand. Though it stung me, I

retained it and looked it over, and in the process was stung several times; but the pain was slight. I saw it was one of our native wild bees, cousin to the leaf-rollers, that build their nests under stones and in decayed fence-rails. (In Packard I found it described under the name of *Andrena*.) Then I inserted a small weed-stalk into one of the holes, and, with a little trowel I carried, proceeded to dig out the nest. The hole was about a foot deep; at the bottom of it I found a little semi-transparent, membranous sac or cell, a little larger than that of the honey-bee; in this sac was a little pellet of yellow pollen—a loaf of bread for the young grub when the egg should have hatched. I explored other nests and found them all the same. This discovery was not a great addition to my sum of natural knowledge, but it was something. Now when I see the signs in a field, I know what they mean: they indicate the tiny earthen cradles of *Andrena*.

Near by I chanced to spy a large hole in the turf, with no mound of soil about it. I could put the end of my little finger into it. I peered down, and saw the gleam of two small, bead-like eyes. I knew it to be the den of the wolf-spider. Was she waiting for some blundering insect to tumble in? I say she, because the real ogre among the spiders is the female. The male is small and of little consequence. A few days later I paused by this den again and saw the members of the ogress scattered about her own door. Had some insect Jack the Giant-Killer been there, or had a still more formidable ogress, the sand-hornet, dragged her forth and carried away her limbless body to her den in the bank?

What the wolf-spider does with the earth it excavates in making its den is a mystery. There is no sign of it anywhere about. Does it force its way down by pushing the soil to one side and packing it there firmly? The entrance to the hole usually has a slight rim or hem to keep the edge from crumbling in.

As it happened, I chanced upon another interesting footnote that very day. I was on my way to a muck swamp in the woods, to see if the showy lady's-slipper was in bloom. Just on the margin of the swamp, in the deep shade of the hemlocks, my eye took note of some small, unshapely creature crawling hurriedly over the ground. I stooped down, and saw it was some large species of moth just out of its case, and in a great hurry to find a suitable place in which to hang itself up and give its wings a chance to unfold before the air dried them. I thrust a small twig in its way, which it instantly seized upon. I lifted it gently, carried it to drier ground, and fixed the stick in the fork of a tree, so that the moth hung free a few feet from the ground. Its body was distended nearly to the size of one's little finger, and surmounted by wings that were so crumpled and stubby that they seemed quite

rudimentary. The creature evidently knew what it wanted, and knew the importance of haste. Instantly these rude, stubby wings began to grow. It was a slow process, but one could see the change from minute to minute. As the wings expanded, the body contracted. By some kind of pumping arrangement air was being forced from a reservoir in the one into the tubes of the other. The wings were not really growing, as they at first seemed to be, but they were unfolding and expanding under this pneumatic pressure from the body. In the course of about half an hour the process was completed, and the winged creature hung there in all its full-fledged beauty. Its color was checked black and white like a loon's back, but its name I know not. My chief interest in it, aside from the interest we feel in any new form of life, arose from the creature's extreme anxiety to reach a perch where it could unfold its wings. A little delay would doubtless have been fatal to it. I wonder how many human geniuses are hatched whose wings are blighted by some accident or untoward circumstance. Or do the wings of genius always unfold, no matter what the environment may be?

One seldom takes a walk without encountering some of this fine print on nature's page. Now it is a little yellowish-white moth that spreads itself upon the middle of a leaf as if to imitate the droppings of birds; or it is the young cicadas working up out of the ground, and in the damp, cool places building little chimneys or tubes above the surface to get more warmth and hasten their development; or it is a wood-newt gorging a tree-cricket, or a small snake gorging the newt,

or a bird song with some striking peculiarity—a strange defect, or a rare excellence. Now it is a shrike impaling his victim, or blue jays mocking and teasing a hawk and dropping quickly into the branches to avoid his angry blows, or a robin hustling a cuckoo out of the tree where her nest is, or a vireo driving away a cowbird, or the partridge blustering about your feet till her young are hidden. One October morning I was walking along the road on the edge of the woods, when I came into a gentle shower of butternuts; one of them struck my hat-brim. I paused and looked about me; here one fell, there another, yonder a third. There was no wind blowing, and I wondered what was loosening the butternuts. Turning my attention to the top of the tree, I soon saw the explanation: a red squirrel was at work gathering his harvest. He would seize a nut, give it a twist, when down it would come; then he would dart to another and another. Farther along I found where he had covered the ground with chestnut burs; he could not wait for the frost and the winds; did he know that the burs would dry and open upon the ground, and that the bitter covering of the butternuts would soon fall away from the nut?

There are three things that perhaps happen near me each season that I have never yet seen—the toad casting its skin, the snake swallowing it's young, and the larva of the moth and butterfly constructing their shrouds. It is a mooted question whether or not the snake does swallow its young, but if there is no other good reason for it, may they not retreat into their mother's stomach to feed? How else are they to be nourished? That the moth larva can weave its own cocoon and attach it to a twig seems more incredible. Yesterday, in my walk, I found a firm, silver-gray cocoon, about two inches long and shaped like an Egyptian mummy (probably *Promethean*), suspended from a branch of a bush by a narrow, stout ribbon twice as long as itself. The fastening was woven around the limb, upon which it turned as if it grew there. I would have given something to have seen the creature perform this feat, and then incase itself so snugly in the silken shroud at the end of this tether. By swinging free, its firm, compact case was in no danger from woodpeckers, as it might have been if resting directly upon a branch or treetrunk. Near by was the cocoon of another species (*Cecropia*) that was fastened directly to the limb; but this was vague, loose, and much more involved and net-like. I have seen the downy woodpecker assaulting one of these cocoons, but its yielding surface and webby interior seemed to puzzle and baffle him.

I am interested even in the way each climbing plant or vine goes up the pole, whether from right to left, or from left to right,—that is, with the hands of a clock or against them,—whether it is under the law of the great cyclonic storms of the northern hemisphere, which all move against the hands of a clock, or in the contrary direction, like the cyclones in the southern hemisphere. I take pleasure in noting every little dancing whirlwind of a summer day that catches up the dust or the leaves before me, and every little funnel-shaped whirlpool in the swollen stream or river, whether or not they spin from right to left or the reverse. If I were in the southern hemisphere, I am sure I should note whether these things were under the law of its cyclones in this respect or under the law of ours. As a rule, our twining plants and toy whirlwinds copy our revolving storms and go against the hands of the clock. But there are exceptions. While the bean, the bittersweet, the morning-glory, and others go up from left to right, the hop, the wild buckwheat, and some others

go up from right to left. Most of our forest trees show a tendency to wind one way or the other, the hard woods going in one direction, and the hemlocks and pines and cedars and butternuts and chestnuts in another. In different localities, or on different geological formations, I find these directions reversed. I recall one instance in the case of a hemlock six or seven inches in diameter, where this tendency to twist had come out of the grain, as it were, and shaped the outward form of the tree, causing it to make, in an ascent of about thirty feet, one complete revolution about a larger tree close to which it grew. On a smaller scale I have seen the same thing in a pine.

Persons lost in the woods or on the plains, or traveling at night, tend, I believe, toward the left. The movements of men and women, it is said, differ in this respect, one sex turning to the right and the other to the left. I had lived in the world more than fifty years before I noticed a peculiarity about the rays of light one often sees diverging from an opening, or a series of openings, in the clouds, namely, that they are like spokes in a wheel, the hub, or center, of which appears to be just there in the vapory masses, instead of being, as is really the case, nearly ninety-three millions of miles beyond. The beams of light that come through cracks or chinks in a wall do not converge in this way, but to

24

the eye run parallel to one another. There is another fact: this fan-shaped display of converging rays is always immediately in front of the observer; that is, exactly between him and the sun, so that the central spoke or shaft in his front is always perpendicular. You cannot see this fan to the right or left of the sun, but only between you and it. Hence, as in the case of the rainbow, no two persons see exactly the same rays.

The eye sees what it has the means of seeing, and its means of seeing are in proportion to the love and desire behind it. The eye is informed and sharpened by the thought. My boy sees ducks on the river where and when I cannot, because at certain seasons he thinks ducks and dreams ducks. One season my neighbor asked me if the bees had injured my grapes. I said, "No; the bees never injure my grapes."

"They do mine," he replied; "they puncture the skin for the juice, and at times the clusters are covered with them."

"No," I said, "it is not the bees that puncture the skin; it is the birds."

"What birds?"

"The orioles."

"But I haven't seen any orioles," he rejoined.

"We have," I continued, "because at this season we think orioles; we have learned by experience how destructive these birds are in the

vineyard, and we are on the lookout for them; our eyes and ears are ready for them."

If we think birds, we shall see birds wherever we go; if we think arrowheads, as Thoreau did, we shall pick up arrowheads in every field. Some people have an eye for four-leaved clovers; they see them as they walk hastily over the turf, for they already have them in their eyes. I once took a walk with the late Professor Eaton of Yale. He was just then specially interested in the mosses, and he found them, all kinds, everywhere. I can see him yet, every few minutes upon his knees, adjusting his eye-glasses before some rare specimen. The beauty he found in them, and pointed out to me, kindled my enthusiasm also. I once spent a summer day at the mountain home of a well-known literary woman and editor. She lamented the absence of birds about her house. I named a half-dozen or more I had heard or seen in her trees within an hour—the indigo-bird, the purple finch, the yellowbird, the very thrush, the red-eyed vireo, the song sparrow.

"Do you mean to say you have seen or heard all these birds while sitting here on my porch?" she inquired.

"I really have," I said.

"I do not see them or hear them," she replied, "and yet I want to very much."

"No," said I; "you only *want to want* to see and hear them."

You must have the bird in your heart before you can find it in the bush.

I was sitting in front of a farmhouse one day in company with the local Nimrod. In a maple tree in front of us I saw the great crested fly-catcher. I called the hunter's attention to it, and asked him if he had ever seen that bird before. No, he had not; it was a new bird to him. But he probably had seen it scores of times,—seen it without regarding it. It was not the game he was in quest of, and his eye heeded it not.

Human and artificial sounds and objects thrust themselves upon us; they are within our sphere, so to speak: but the life of nature we must meet halfway; it is shy, withdrawn, and blends itself with a vast neutral background. We must be initiated; it is an order the secrets of which are well guarded.

Spring

S pring is an exhilarating season. There is activity everywhere— bare branches of trees erupting in new growth, plants bursting triumphant from the soil, flowers flinging wide their petals to embrace the sun. Birds flaunt their flashiest feathers and sing loud their sweetest songs. This is a time of birth, renewal, and fresh starts. What a marvelous opportunity to set some new intentions. Write down a few short term goals and outline a realistic plan for achieving them. Make an effort to really open yourself up, both mentally and emotionally, to new possibilities. They are all around you!

"Meditation and water are wedded forever."
—Herman Melville

Signs of Spring

- O Hummingbird nests
- O Cherry blossoms
- O Cactus flowers blooming
- O Fiddlehead ferns
- O Ramps
- O Robins' eggs
- O Ripe mulberries
- O Orange blossoms
- O Migrating songbirds
- O Pussy willows

Date

. . . .

Time of Day

. . . .

Nature Observations

. . . .

. . . .

. . . .

. . . .

. . . .

. . . .

Thoughts on Spring

. . . .

. . . .

. . . .

. . . .

. . . .

. . . .

. . . .

Date

. . . .

Time of Day

. . . .

Nature Observations

. . . .

. . . .

. . . .

. . . .

. . . .

. . . .

Thoughts on Spring

. . . .

. . . .

. . . .

. . . .

. . . .

. . . .

. . . .

. . . .

Date

Time of Day

Nature Observations

Thoughts on Spring

Date

....

Time of Day

....

Nature Observations

....

....

....

....

....

....

....

Thoughts on Spring

....

....

....

....

....

....

....

....

Date
....

Time of Day
....

Nature Observations
....

....

....

....

....

....

Thoughts on Spring
....

....

....

....

....

....

....

....

Date

....

Time of Day

....

Nature Observations

....

....

....

....

....

....

Thoughts on Spring

....

....

....

....

....

....

....

....

Date

....

Time of Day

....

Nature Observations

....

....

....

....

....

....

Thoughts on Spring

....

....

....

....

....

....

....

....

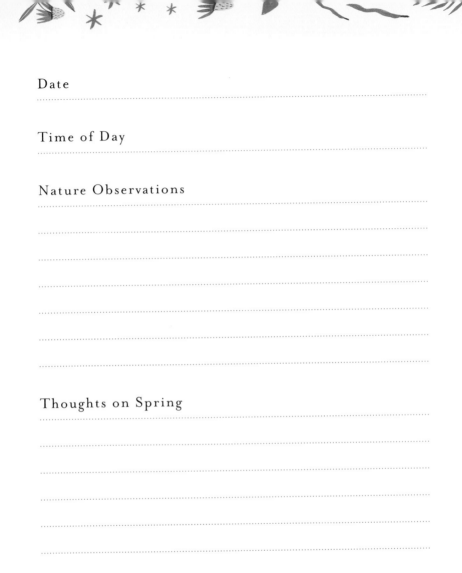

Date
....

Time of Day
....

Nature Observations
....
....
....
....
....
....
....

Thoughts on Spring
....
....
....
....
....
....
....
....

Date

. . . .

Time of Day

. . . .

Nature Observations

. . . .

. . . .

. . . .

. . . .

. . . .

Thoughts on Spring

. . . .

. . . .

. . . .

. . . .

. . . .

. . . .

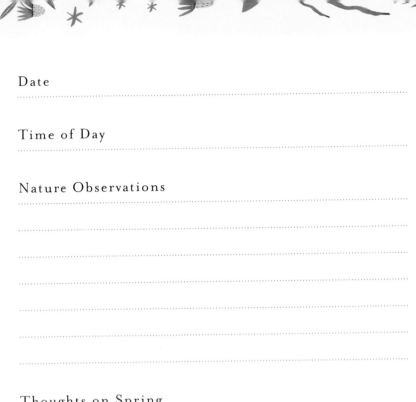

Date

Time of Day

Nature Observations

Thoughts on Spring

Date

....

Time of Day

....

Nature Observations

....

....

....

....

....

....

Thoughts on Spring

....

....

....

....

....

....

....

....

Date
....

Time of Day
....

Nature Observations
....
....
....
....
....
....
....

Thoughts on Spring
....
....
....
....
....
....
....
....
....

Date

....

Time of Day

....

Nature Observations

....

....

....

....

....

Thoughts on Spring

....

....

....

....

....

....

....

....

Date

Time of Day

Nature Observations

Thoughts on Spring

Date

....

Time of Day

....

Nature Observations

....

....

....

....

....

....

Thoughts on Spring

....

....

....

....

....

....

....

....

....

Date

....

Time of Day

....

Nature Observations

....

....

....

....

....

....

Thoughts on Spring

....

....

....

....

....

....

....

....

Date

....

Time of Day

....

Nature Observations

....

....

....

....

....

....

Thoughts on Spring

....

....

....

....

....

....

....

....

Date

....

Time of Day

....

Nature Observations

....

....

....

....

....

....

....

Thoughts on Spring

....

....

....

....

....

....

....

....

Date

....

Time of Day

....

Nature Observations

....

....

....

....

....

....

....

Thoughts on Spring

....

....

....

....

....

....

....

....

....

Date

....

Time of Day

....

Nature Observations

....

....

....

....

....

....

Thoughts on Spring

....

....

....

....

....

....

....

....

Date

Time of Day

Nature Observations

Thoughts on Spring

Date
....

Time of Day
....

Nature Observations
....

....

....

....

....

....

Thoughts on Spring
....

....

....

....

....

....

....

....

Date

....

Time of Day

....

Nature Observations

....

....

....

....

....

....

Thoughts on Spring

....

....

....

....

....

....

....

....

Date

....

Time of Day

....

Nature Observations

....

....

....

....

....

....

Thoughts on Spring

....

....

....

....

....

....

....

....

Date

....

Time of Day

....

Nature Observations

....

....

....

....

....

....

Thoughts on Spring

....

....

....

....

....

....

....

....

Date

....

Time of Day

....

Nature Observations

....

....

....

....

....

....

....

Thoughts on Spring

....

....

....

....

....

....

....

....

Date

....

Time of Day

....

Nature Observations

....

....

....

....

....

....

Thoughts on Spring

....

....

....

....

....

....

....

....

....

Date

....

Time of Day

....

Nature Observations

....

....

....

....

....

....

....

Thoughts on Spring

....

....

....

....

....

....

....

....

Date
....

Time of Day
....

Nature Observations
....

....

....

....

....

....

Thoughts on Spring
....

....

....

....

....

....

....

....

Date

....

Time of Day

....

Nature Observations

....

....

....

....

....

....

Thoughts on Spring

....

....

....

....

....

....

....

Date

....

Time of Day

....

Nature Observations

....

....

....

....

....

Thoughts on Spring

....

....

....

....

....

....

....

Date

. . . .

Time of Day

. . . .

Nature Observations

. . . .

. . . .

. . . .

. . . .

. . . .

. . . .

Thoughts on Spring

. . . .

. . . .

. . . .

. . . .

. . . .

. . . .

. . . .

Date
....

Time of Day
....

Nature Observations
....

....

....

....

....

....

Thoughts on Spring
....

....

....

....

....

....

....

....

Date

....

Time of Day

....

Nature Observations

....

....

....

....

....

....

Thoughts on Spring

....

....

....

....

....

....

....

....

Date
....

Time of Day
....

Nature Observations
....

....

....

....

....

....

Thoughts on Spring
....

....

....

....

....

....

....

....

Date

....

Time of Day

....

Nature Observations

....

....

....

....

....

....

....

Thoughts on Spring

....

....

....

....

....

....

....

....

Date

....

Time of Day

....

Nature Observations

....

....

....

....

....

....

Thoughts on Spring

....

....

....

....

....

....

....

....

Summer

Slow down and luxuriate in the lush, leafy vibrance of summer. With lengthening days and climbing temperatures, summer lends itself to close observation and leisurely contemplation. Revel in the simple symmetry of a melon, bask in the rich colors of ripe berries, savor the bright clean flavor of an ear of sweet corn. It's a great time for bold decisions and fun adventures. Make affirmative lists: what do you like best about yourself, what are some things you are good at, what makes you a valuable friend? Greet each day with an attitude of YES and enjoy the resulting serendipity.

Gazing up at the sky during a clear summer night can transport you to another world. Wave at the moon. Wink back at the stars. Throw your arms wide and embrace the infinite. Contemplate the vastness of the universe and record your musings in your journal.

" To make a prairie it takes a clover and one bee,
One clover, and a bee,
And revery.
The revery alone will do,
If bees are few. "

—Emily Dickinson

Walt Whitman

from *Specimen Days*, 1892

The author of *Leaves of Grass* (1855), Walt Whitman (1819–1892) was described by Ezra Pound as "America's poet...he is America." *Specimen Days* collects a variety of his free-form observational writing, from Civil War reporting to his own "awakening in the wild" as a suburbanite wandering into the woods.

Birds Migrating at Midnight

Did you ever chance to hear the midnight flight of birds passing through the air and darkness overhead, in countless armies, changing their early or late summer habitat? It is something not to be forgotten. A friend called me up just after 12 last night to mark the peculiar noise of unusually immense flocks migrating north (rather late this year). In the silence, shadow and delicious odor of the hour, (the natural perfume belonging to the night alone,) I thought it rare music. You could hear the characteristic motion—once or twice "the rush of mighty wings," but often a velvety rustle, long drawn out—sometimes quite near—with continual calls and chirps, and some song-notes. It all lasted from 12 till after 3. Once in a while the species was plainly distinguishable; I could make out the bobolink, tanager, Wilson's thrush, white-crown'd sparrow, and occasionally from high in the air came the notes of the plover.

The Lesson of a Tree

Sept. 1.

I should not take either the biggest or the most picturesque tree
to illustrate it. Here is one of my favorites now before me, a fine
yellow poplar, quite straight, perhaps 90 feet high, and four thick at
the butt. How strong, vital, enduring! how dumbly eloquent! What
suggestions of imperturbability and being, as against the human trait
of mere seeming. Then the qualities, almost emotional, palpably
artistic, heroic, of a tree; so innocent and harmless, yet so savage. It
is, yet says nothing. How it rebukes by its tough and equable serenity
all weathers, this gusty-tempered little whiffet, man that runs indoors
at a mite of rain or snow. Science (or rather half-way science) scoffs
at reminiscence of dryad and hamadryad, and of trees speaking.
But, if they don't, they do as well as most speaking, writing, poetry,
sermons—or rather they do a great deal better. I should say indeed
that those old dryad-reminiscences are quite as true as any, and
profounder than most reminiscences we get. ("Cut this out," as the
quack mediciners say, and keep by you.) Go and sit in a grove or
woods, with one or more of those voiceless companions, and read the
foregoing, and think.

One lesson from affiliating a tree—perhaps the greatest moral lesson
anyhow from earth, rocks, animals, is that same lesson of inherency,
of what is, without the least regard to what the looker-on (the critic)
supposes or says, or whether he likes or dislikes. What worse—what more
general malady pervades each and all of us, our literature, education,
attitude toward each other, (even toward ourselves,) than a morbid
trouble about seems, (generally temporarily seems too,) and no trouble

at all, or hardly any, about the sane, slow-growing, perennial, real parts of character, books, friendship, marriage—humanity's invisible foundations and hold-together? (As the all-basis, the nerve, the great-sympathetic, the plenum within humanity, giving stamp to everything, is necessarily invisible.)

Aug. 4. 6 P.M.

Lights and shades and rare effects on tree-foliage and grass—transparent greens, grays, &c., all in sunset pomp and dazzle. The clear beams are now thrown in many new places, on the quilted, seamed, bronze-drab, lower tree-trunks, shadowed except at this hour—now flooding their young and old columnar ruggedness with strong light, unfolding to my sense new amazing features of silent, shaggy charm, the solid bark, the expression of harmless impassiveness, with many a bulge and gnarl untracked before. In the revealing's of such light, such exceptional hour, such mood, one does not wonder at the old story fables, (indeed, why fables?) of people falling into love-sickness with trees, seized ecstatic with the mystic realism of the resistless silent strength in them—strength, which after all is perhaps the last, completest, highest beauty.

Summer Sights and Indulgences

June 10th.

As I write, 5-1/2 P.M., here by the creek, nothing can exceed the quiet splendor and freshness around me. We had a heavy shower, with brief thunder and lightning, in the middle of the day; and since, overhead, one of those not uncommon yet indescribable skies (in quality, not details or forms) of limpid blue, with rolling silver-fringed clouds, and a pure-dazzling sun. For underlay, trees in fullness of tender foliage—liquid, reedy, long-drawn notes of birds—based by the fretful mewing of a querulous cat-bird, and the pleasant chippering-shriek of two kingfishers. I have been watching the latter the last half hour, on their regular evening frolic over and in the stream; evidently a spree of the liveliest kind. They pursue each other, whirling and wheeling around, with many a jocund downward dip, splashing the spray in jets of diamonds—and then off they swoop, with slanting wings and graceful flight, sometimes so near me I can plainly see their dark-gray feather-bodies and milk-white necks.

Sundown Perfume—Quail-Notes—
The Hermit-Thrush

June 19th. 4 to 6-1/2. P.M.

Sitting alone by the creek—solitude here, but the scene bright and vivid enough—the sun shining, and quite a fresh wind blowing (some heavy showers last night,) the grass and trees looking their best—the clare-obscure of different greens, shadows, half-shadows, and the dappling glimpses of the water, through recesses—the wild flageolet-note of a quail near by—the just-heard fretting of some hylas down there in the pond—crows cawing in the distance—a drove of young hogs rooting in soft ground near the oak under which I sit—some come sniffing near me, and then scamper away, with grunts. And still the clear notes of the quail—the quiver of leaf-shadows over the paper as I write—the sky aloft, with white clouds, and the sun well declining to the west—the swift darting of many sand-swallows coming and going, their holes in a neighboring marl-bank—the odor of the cedar and oak, so palpable, as evening approaches—perfume, color, the bronze-and-gold of nearly ripened wheat—clover-fields, with honey-scent—the well-up maize, with long and rustling leaves—the great patches of thriving potatoes, dusky green, flecked all over with white blossoms—the old, warty, venerable oak above me—and ever, mixed with the dual notes of the quail, the soughing of the wind through some near-by pines.

As I rise for return, I linger long to a delicious song-epilogue (is it the hermit-thrush?) from some bushy recess off there in the swamp, repeated leisurely and pensively over and over again. This, to the circle-gambols of the swallows flying by dozens in concentric rings in the last rays of sunset, like flashes of some airy wheel.

Look down; there is a whole world underfoot that often goes unnoticed. Walk barefoot on the grass, and let it tickle your toes. Hunt around for a four-leaf clover. Make a list of all the things that help you feel lucky. What are you grateful for?

Summer Treasures

- ○ Rainbows
- ○ Muscadine grapes
- ○ Fireflies
- ○ Cattails
- ○ Dandelion fluff
- ○ Tadpoles
- ○ Jasmine
- ○ Bats
- ○ Dragonflies
- ○ Bees

Date

Time of Day

Nature Observations

Thoughts on Summer

Date

....

Time of Day

....

Nature Observations

....

....

....

....

....

....

Thoughts on Summer

....

....

....

....

....

....

....

....

Date

....

Time of Day

....

Nature Observations

....

....

....

....

....

....

Thoughts on Summer

....

....

....

....

....

....

....

....

Date

....

Time of Day

....

Nature Observations

....

....

....

....

....

....

Thoughts on Summer

....

....

....

....

....

....

....

Date

....

Time of Day

....

Nature Observations

....

....

....

....

....

....

Thoughts on Summer

....

....

....

....

....

....

....

....

Date

....

Time of Day

....

Nature Observations

....

....

....

....

....

....

Thoughts on Summer

....

....

....

....

....

....

....

....

Date

....

Time of Day

....

Nature Observations

....

....

....

....

....

....

Thoughts on Summer

....

....

....

....

....

....

....

....

Date

....

Time of Day

....

Nature Observations

....

....

....

....

....

....

Thoughts on Summer

....

....

....

....

....

....

....

....

Date

....

Time of Day

....

Nature Observations

....

....

....

....

....

....

Thoughts on Summer

....

....

....

....

....

....

....

....

Date

....

Time of Day

....

Nature Observations

....

....

....

....

....

....

Thoughts on Summer

....

....

....

....

....

....

....

....

Date

....

Time of Day

....

Nature Observations

....

....

....

....

....

....

Thoughts on Summer

....

....

....

....

....

....

....

....

Date

....

Time of Day

....

Nature Observations

....

....

....

....

....

....

Thoughts on Summer

....

....

....

....

....

....

....

....

Date

....

Time of Day

....

Nature Observations

....

....

....

....

....

....

Thoughts on Summer

....

....

....

....

....

....

....

....

Date

....

Time of Day

....

Nature Observations

....

....

....

....

....

....

Thoughts on Summer

....

....

....

....

....

....

....

....

Date

Time of Day

Nature Observations

Thoughts on Summer

Date

Time of Day

Nature Observations

Thoughts on Summer

Date

....

Time of Day

....

Nature Observations

....

....

....

....

....

....

....

Thoughts on Summer

....

....

....

....

....

....

....

....

Date

....

Time of Day

....

Nature Observations

....

....

....

....

....

....

Thoughts on Summer

....

....

....

....

....

....

....

Date

....

Time of Day

....

Nature Observations

....

....

....

....

....

....

Thoughts on Summer

....

....

....

....

....

....

....

....

Date

....

Time of Day

....

Nature Observations

....

....

....

....

....

....

Thoughts on Summer

....

....

....

....

....

....

....

....

Date

....

Time of Day

....

Nature Observations

....

....

....

....

....

....

....

Thoughts on Summer

....

....

....

....

....

....

....

....

Date

....

Time of Day

....

Nature Observations

....

....

....

....

....

....

Thoughts on Summer

....

....

....

....

....

....

....

Date

....

Time of Day

....

Nature Observations

....

....

....

....

....

....

Thoughts on Summer

....

....

....

....

....

....

....

....

Date

....

Time of Day

....

Nature Observations

....

....

....

....

....

....

Thoughts on Summer

....

....

....

....

....

....

....

....

Date

....

Time of Day

....

Nature Observations

....

....

....

....

....

....

....

Thoughts on Summer

....

....

....

....

....

....

....

....

Date

....

Time of Day

....

Nature Observations

....

....

....

....

....

....

Thoughts on Summer

....

....

....

....

....

....

....

....

Date

....

Time of Day

....

Nature Observations

....

....

....

....

....

....

Thoughts on Summer

....

....

....

....

....

....

....

....

Date

....

Time of Day

....

Nature Observations

....

....

....

....

....

....

Thoughts on Summer

....

....

....

....

....

....

....

....

Date

....

Time of Day

....

Nature Observations

....

....

....

....

....

....

Thoughts on Summer

....

....

....

....

....

....

....

....

Date

....

Time of Day

....

Nature Observations

....

....

....

....

....

....

Thoughts on Summer

....

....

....

....

....

....

....

....

Date

Time of Day

Nature Observations

Thoughts on Summer

Date

....

Time of Day

....

Nature Observations

....

....

....

....

....

....

Thoughts on Summer

....

....

....

....

....

....

....

Autumn

A utumn is a season of splendor. Leaves go from deep green to dazzling shades of orange, yellow, and red, each tree igniting into its own dreamy blaze. Crisp apples, ripe for the picking, dangle from branches, all but begging to be transformed into pie. Squirrels scurry about, taking advantage of the season's abundance by stockpiling seeds and nuts. Monarch butterflies and birds embark upon epic migrations, proving with every wing beat that nothing is impossible. This is an ideal time to focus on self-improvement. Take a gentle personal inventory— is there any aspect of your life, big or small, that you wish was different? Remember to be kind with yourself, do not indulge in harsh or critical self evaluation. Self love is key to finding the courage to make changes.

" Through woods and mountain passes
The winds, like anthems, roll. "
—Henry Wadsworth Longfellow

Walt Whitman

from *Specimen Days*, 1892

Though Whitman himself described it as a "prose jumble," *Specimen Days* gives us a unique view into the poet's life. His retreat to the country happened after the Civil War and during his later years, and his meditations on nature display a therapy for the soul. In his musings on Autumn, Whitman sees the changing seasons and dying year as embodying his own old age, a time of quiet transformation and reflection after a long and busy life.

Autumn Side-Bits

Oct. 1, 2 and 3.

Down every day in the solitude of the creek. A serene autumn sun and westerly breeze to-day (3d) as I sit here, the water surface prettily moving in wind-ripples before me. On a stout old beech at the edge, decayed and slanting, almost fallen to the stream, yet with life and leaves in its mossy limbs, a gray squirrel, exploring, runs up and down, flirts his tail, leaps to the ground, sits on his haunches upright as he sees me, (a Darwinian hint?) and then races up the tree again.

Oct. 4.

Cloudy and coolish; signs of incipient winter. Yet pleasant here, the leaves thick-falling, the ground brown with them already; rich coloring, yellows of all hues, pale and dark-green, shades from lightest to richest red—all set in and toned down by the prevailing brown of the earth and gray of the sky. So, winter is coming; and I yet in my sickness. I sit here amid all these fair sights and vital influences, and abandon myself to that thought, with its wandering trains of speculation.

The Sky—Days and Nights—Happiness

Oct. 20

A clear, crispy day—dry and breezy air, full of oxygen. Out of the sane, silent, beauteous miracles that envelope and fuse me—trees, water, grass, sunlight, and early frost—the one I am looking at most to-day is the sky. It has that delicate, transparent blue, peculiar to autumn, and the only clouds are little or larger white ones, giving their still and spiritual motion to the great concave. All through the earlier day (say from 7 to 11) it keeps a pure, yet vivid blue. But as noon approaches the color gets lighter, quite gray for two or three hours—then still paler for a spell, till sun-down—which last I watch dazzling through the interstices of a knoll of big trees—darts of fire and a gorgeous show of light-yellow, liver-color and red, with a vast silver glaze ascent on the water—the transparent shadows, shafts, sparkle, and vivid colors beyond all the paintings ever made.

COLORS—A CONTRAST

Such a play of colors and lights, different seasons, different hours of the day—the lines of the far horizon where the faint-tinged edge of the landscape loses itself in the sky. As I slowly hobble up the lane toward day-close, an incomparable sunset shooting in molten sapphire and gold, shaft after shaft, through the ranks of the long-leaved corn, between me and the west. Another day—The rich dark green of the tulip-trees and the oaks, the gray of the swamp-willows, the dull hues of the sycamores and black-walnuts, the emerald of the cedars (after rain,) and the light yellow of the beeches.

Wind can sound like voices rising and falling is gusty conversation as fallen leaves blow chattering along sidewalks. Close your eyes and listen closely. What is the wind saying to you? Watch the bare branches of trees be tossed back and forth. What messages are they spelling out across the sky? Write it all down.

Hints of Autumn

- ○ *Squirrels hiding nuts*
- ○ *Birds flying south in a V formation*
- ○ *Monarch butterflies*
- ○ *Ripe apples in trees*
- ○ *Pumpkin patches*
- ○ *Leaves changing color*
- ○ *Sycamore seed "helicopters"*
- ○ *Acorns*
- ○ *Mushrooms*
- ○ *Ladybugs indoors*

Date

....

Time of Day

....

Nature Observations

....

....

....

....

....

....

Thoughts on Autumn

....

....

....

....

....

....

....

....

Date

Time of Day

Nature Observations

Thoughts on Autumn

Date

....

Time of Day

....

Nature Observations

....

....

....

....

....

....

Thoughts on Autumn

....

....

....

....

....

....

....

....

Date

....

Time of Day

....

Nature Observations

....

....

....

....

....

Thoughts on Autumn

....

....

....

....

....

....

....

....

Date

....

Time of Day

....

Nature Observations

....

....

....

....

....

....

Thoughts on Autumn

....

....

....

....

....

....

....

....

Date

Time of Day

Nature Observations

Thoughts on Autumn

Date

....

Time of Day

....

Nature Observations

....

....

....

....

....

....

....

Thoughts on Autumn

....

....

....

....

....

....

....

....

Date

....

Time of Day

....

Nature Observations

....

....

....

....

....

....

....

Thoughts on Autumn

....

....

....

....

....

....

....

....

Date

....

Time of Day

....

Nature Observations

....

....

....

....

....

....

Thoughts on Autumn

....

....

....

....

....

....

....

....

Date

....

Time of Day

....

Nature Observations

....

....

....

....

....

....

Thoughts on Autumn

....

....

....

....

....

....

....

....

Date

....

Time of Day

....

Nature Observations

....

....

....

....

....

Thoughts on Autumn

....

....

....

....

....

....

....

....

Date

....

Time of Day

....

Nature Observations

....

....

....

....

....

....

Thoughts on Autumn

....

....

....

....

....

....

....

....

133

Date

....

Time of Day

....

Nature Observations

....

....

....

....

....

....

Thoughts on Autumn

....

....

....

....

....

....

....

....

Date

....

Time of Day

....

Nature Observations

....

....

....

....

....

....

Thoughts on Autumn

....

....

....

....

....

....

....

....

Date

....

Time of Day

....

Nature Observations

....

....

....

....

....

....

....

Thoughts on Autumn

....

....

....

....

....

....

....

....

Date

....

Time of Day

....

Nature Observations

....

....

....

....

....

....

Thoughts on Autumn

....

....

....

....

....

....

....

....

Date

....

Time of Day

....

Nature Observations

....

....

....

....

....

....

Thoughts on Autumn

....

....

....

....

....

....

....

....

Date

....

Time of Day

....

Nature Observations

....

....

....

....

....

....

Thoughts on Autumn

....

....

....

....

....

....

....

....

Date

....

Time of Day

....

Nature Observations

....

....

....

....

....

....

....

Thoughts on Autumn

....

....

....

....

....

....

....

....

Date

....

Time of Day

....

Nature Observations

....

....

....

....

....

....

Thoughts on Autumn

....

....

....

....

....

....

....

....

141

Date

....

Time of Day

....

Nature Observations

....

....

....

....

....

....

Thoughts on Autumn

....

....

....

....

....

....

....

....

Date

....

Time of Day

....

Nature Observations

....

....

....

....

....

....

Thoughts on Autumn

....

....

....

....

....

....

....

....

Date

....

Time of Day

....

Nature Observations

....

....

....

....

....

....

Thoughts on Autumn

....

....

....

....

....

....

....

....

Date

....

Time of Day

....

Nature Observations

....

....

....

....

....

....

Thoughts on Autumn

....

....

....

....

....

....

....

....

....

Date

....

Time of Day

....

Nature Observations

....

....

....

....

....

....

Thoughts on Autumn

....

....

....

....

....

....

....

....

Date

....

Time of Day

....

Nature Observations

....

....

....

....

....

....

Thoughts on Autumn

....

....

....

....

....

....

....

....

Date

....

Time of Day

....

Nature Observations

....

....

....

....

....

....

....

Thoughts on Autumn

....

....

....

....

....

....

....

....

Date

. . . .

Time of Day

. . . .

Nature Observations

. . . .

. . . .

. . . .

. . . .

. . . .

Thoughts on Autumn

. . . .

. . . .

. . . .

. . . .

. . . .

. . . .

. . . .

Date

....

Time of Day

....

Nature Observations

....

....

....

....

....

....

Thoughts on Autumn

....

....

....

....

....

....

....

....

Date

....

Time of Day

....

Nature Observations

....

....

....

....

....

....

Thoughts on Autumn

....

....

....

....

....

....

....

....

Date

....

Time of Day

....

Nature Observations

....

....

....

....

....

....

....

Thoughts on Autumn

....

....

....

....

....

....

....

....

....

Date

....

Time of Day

....

Nature Observations

....

....

....

....

....

Thoughts on Autumn

....

....

....

....

....

....

....

Date

....

Time of Day

....

Nature Observations

....

....

....

....

....

....

....

Thoughts on Autumn

....

....

....

....

....

....

....

....

Date

....

Time of Day

....

Nature Observations

....

....

....

....

....

....

....

Thoughts on Autumn

....

....

....

....

....

....

....

....

Date

....

Time of Day

....

Nature Observations

....

....

....

....

....

....

Thoughts on Autumn

....

....

....

....

....

....

....

....

Date

....

Time of Day

....

Nature Observations

....

....

....

....

....

....

Thoughts on Autumn

....

....

....

....

....

....

....

....

Date

....

Time of Day

....

Nature Observations

....

....

....

....

....

....

Thoughts on Autumn

....

....

....

....

....

....

....

....

Date

....

Time of Day

....

Nature Observations

....

....

....

....

....

....

Thoughts on Autumn

....

....

....

....

....

....

....

....

Winter

❝ T is the season to seek out a safe, cozy spot, curl up, and find some quiet peace. So many plants and animals find ways to hunker down and conserve energy during these harsher winter months. The meditative stillness that is inherent in the shorter days and longer nights provides a nurturing environment in which to work on building inner strength and harmony. Visualize snow falling and drifting to cover all the negativity in your life like a pristine, white blanket. Then imagine it melting away and taking all the thoughts and feelings you are ready to be rid of along with it. By consciously reflecting upon and then letting go of any baggage that may be weighing you down spiritually and emotionally, you will create space for new feelings, new opportunities, and new experiences.

"Look up at the miracle of the falling snow,
—the air a dizzy maze of whirling, eddying flakes, noiselessly transforming
the world, the exquisite crystals dropping in ditch and gutter, and disguising
in the same suit of spotless livery all objects upon which they fall"

— John Burroughs, "The Snow-Walkers", 1876

Watching snow swirl and drift outside from a cozy spot indoors is meditative all on its own. Marvel at the fact that no two snowflakes are alike, then begin to reflect upon your own uniqueness. What qualities do you possess that make you unlike everyone else? This is not a time for modesty or self-deprecation, this is time for you to trumpet your own horn. Toot loud, toot proud! Make a list. Keep adding to it. You are amazing.

Winter's Gifts

- ○ Pinecones
- ○ Aurora Borealis (Northern Lights)
- ○ Icicles
- ○ Evergreens
- ○ Owls
- ○ Snowshoe hares
- ○ Holly berries
- ○ Frost patterns on windows

Date

....

Time of Day

....

Nature Observations

....

....

....

....

....

Thoughts on Winter

....

....

....

....

....

....

....

....

....

Date

Time of Day

Nature Observations

Thoughts on Winter

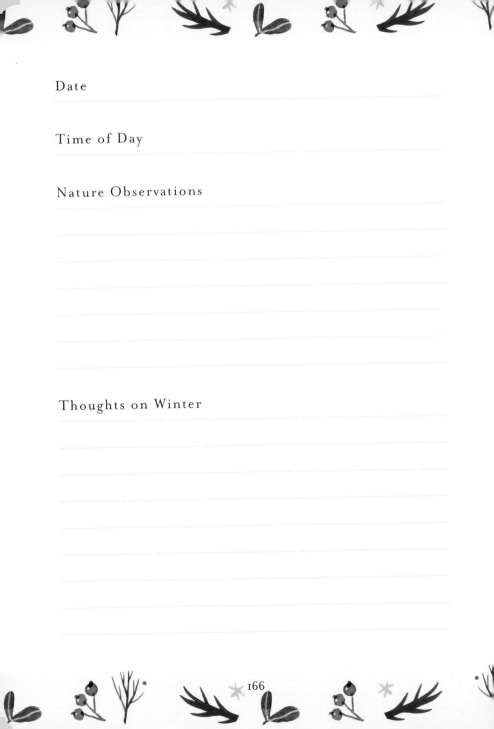

Date
....

Time of Day
....

Nature Observations
....

....

....

....

....

....

Thoughts on Winter
....

....

....

....

....

....

....

....

Date

....

Time of Day

....

Nature Observations

....

....

....

....

....

....

Thoughts on Winter

....

....

....

....

....

....

....

....

Date

....

Time of Day

....

Nature Observations

....

....

....

....

....

....

....

Thoughts on Winter

....

....

....

....

....

....

....

....

....

Date

Time of Day

Nature Observations

Thoughts on Winter

Date

Time of Day

Nature Observations

Thoughts on Winter

Date

....

Time of Day

....

Nature Observations

....

....

....

....

....

....

Thoughts on Winter

....

....

....

....

....

....

....

....

Date

Time of Day

Nature Observations

Thoughts on Winter

Date

....

Time of Day

....

Nature Observations

....

....

....

....

....

....

Thoughts on Winter

....

....

....

....

....

....

....

....

Date

....

Time of Day

....

Nature Observations

....

....

....

....

....

....

Thoughts on Winter

....

....

....

....

....

....

....

....

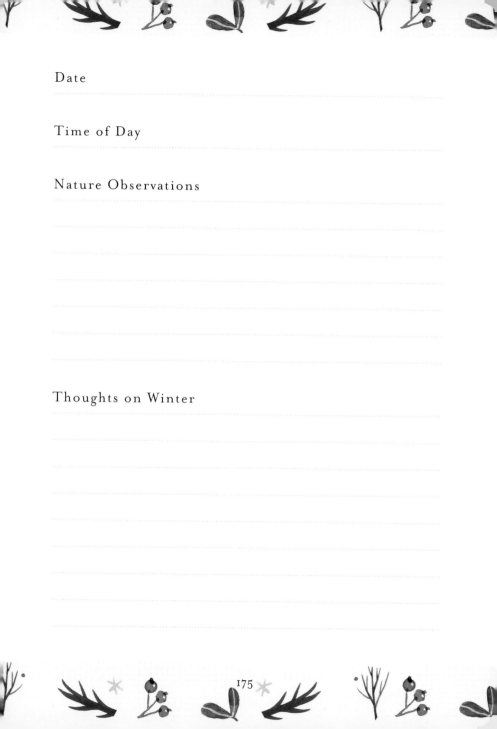

Date

Time of Day

Nature Observations

Thoughts on Winter

Date

....

Time of Day

....

Nature Observations

....

....

....

....

....

....

Thoughts on Winter

....

....

....

....

....

....

....

....

Date

....

Time of Day

....

Nature Observations

....

....

....

....

....

....

Thoughts on Winter

....

....

....

....

....

....

....

....

Date

....

Time of Day

....

Nature Observations

....

....

....

....

....

....

....

Thoughts on Winter

....

....

....

....

....

....

....

....

....

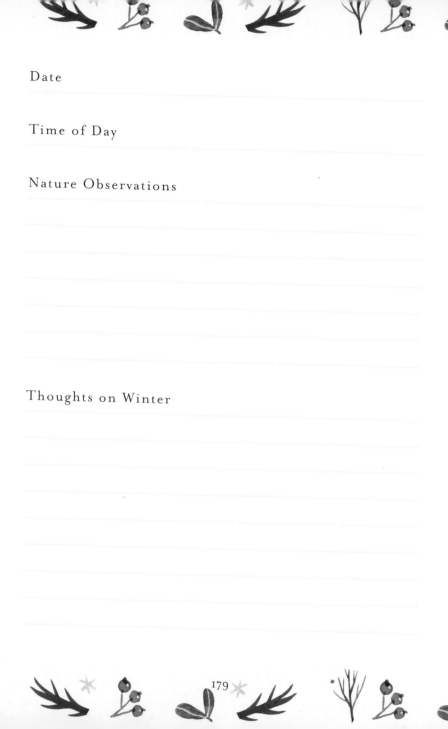

Date

Time of Day

Nature Observations

Thoughts on Winter

Date

Time of Day

Nature Observations

Thoughts on Winter

Date

Time of Day

Nature Observations

Thoughts on Winter

Date

....

Time of Day

....

Nature Observations

....

....

....

....

....

....

....

Thoughts on Winter

....

....

....

....

....

....

....

....

Date

....

Time of Day

....

Nature Observations

....

....

....

....

....

....

Thoughts on Winter

....

....

....

....

....

....

....

....

Date

Time of Day

Nature Observations

Thoughts on Winter

Date

Time of Day

Nature Observations

Thoughts on Winter

Date

Time of Day

Nature Observations

Thoughts on Winter

Date

....

Time of Day

....

Nature Observations

....

....

....

....

....

....

Thoughts on Winter

....

....

....

....

....

....

....

....

....

Date
....

Time of Day
....

Nature Observations
....

....

....

....

....

....

Thoughts on Winter
....

....

....

....

....

....

....

....

Date

....

Time of Day

....

Nature Observations

....

....

....

....

....

....

Thoughts on Winter

....

....

....

....

....

....

....

....

Date

Time of Day

Nature Observations

Thoughts on Winter

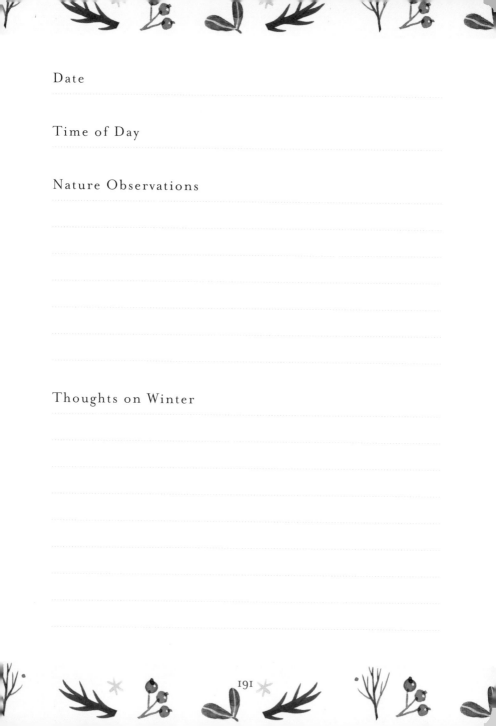

Date

....

Time of Day

....

Nature Observations

....

....

....

....

....

....

Thoughts on Winter

....

....

....

....

....

....

....

....

Date

Time of Day

Nature Observations

Thoughts on Winter

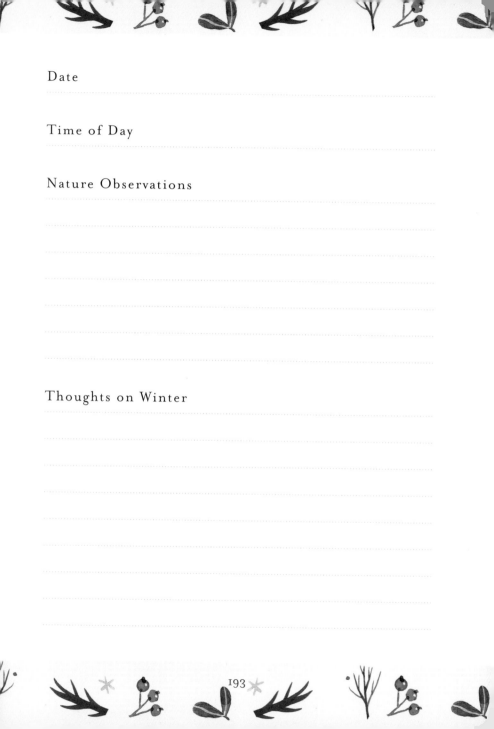

Date

Time of Day

Nature Observations

Thoughts on Winter

Date

....

Time of Day

....

Nature Observations

....

....

....

....

....

....

Thoughts on Winter

....

....

....

....

....

....

....

....

Date

....

Time of Day

....

Nature Observations

....

....

....

....

....

....

Thoughts on Winter

....

....

....

....

....

....

....

....

....

Date

....

Time of Day

....

Nature Observations

....

....

....

....

....

....

Thoughts on Winter

....

....

....

....

....

....

....

....

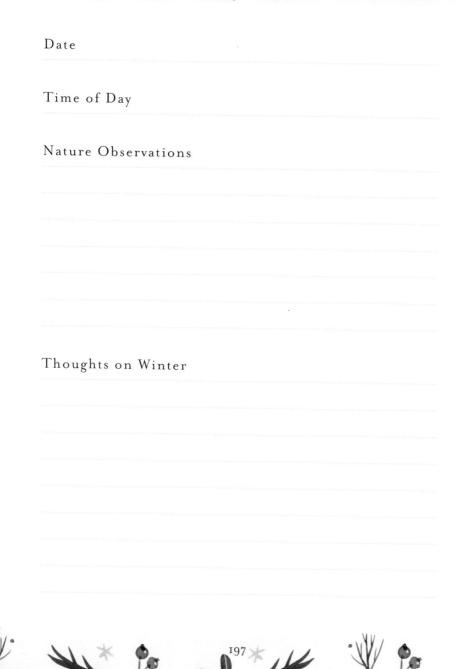

Date

Time of Day

Nature Observations

Thoughts on Winter

Date

Time of Day

Nature Observations

Thoughts on Winter

Date

....

Time of Day

....

Nature Observations

....

....

....

....

....

....

Thoughts on Winter

....

....

....

....

....

....

....

....

Date

Time of Day

Nature Observations

Thoughts on Winter

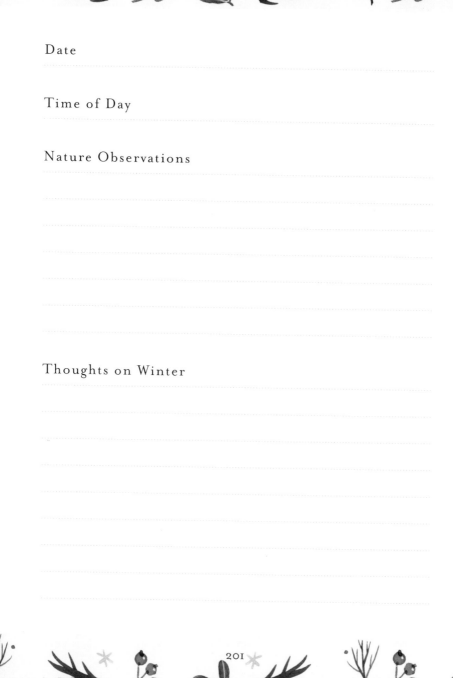

Date
....

Time of Day
....

Nature Observations
....

....

....

....

....

....

Thoughts on Winter
....

....

....

....

....

....

....

....

Date

....

Time of Day

....

Nature Observations

....

....

....

....

....

....

Thoughts on Winter

....

....

....

....

....

....

....

....

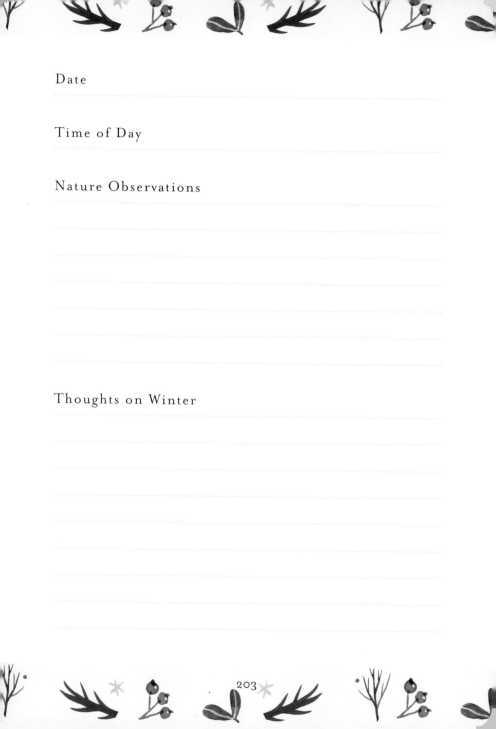

Date

Time of Day

Nature Observations

Thoughts on Winter

Date

Time of Day

Nature Observations

Thoughts on Winter

Date

....

Time of Day

....

Nature Observations

....

....

....

....

....

....

Thoughts on Winter

....

....

....

....

....

....

....

....

Date

Time of Day

Nature Observations

Thoughts on Winter

Date

....

Time of Day

....

Nature Observations

....

....

....

....

....

Thoughts on Winter

....

....

....

....

....

....

....

....

Citations

Burroughs, John. *Leaf and Tendril.* New York: Houghton, Mifflin Company. 1908. Archive.org. Web. September 2016.

Burroughs, John. "The Snow-Walkers." *Winter Sunshine.* New York: Hurd and Houghton, 1876. Google Books. Web. September 2016.

Dickinson, Emily. "XXXIV," *The Complete Poems of Emily Dickinson.* Boston: Little, Brown, and Company, 1924. Bartleby. Web. September 2016.

Longfellow, Henry Wadsworth. "Midnight Mass for the Dying Year." *The Poetical Works of Henry Wadsworth Longfellow.* Boston: Houghton Mifflin Company, 1863. Google Books. Web. September 2016.

Melville, Herman. *Moby-Dick, or The Whale.* London: Constable, and Co., 1922. Bartleby. Web. September 2016.

Thoreau, Henry David. "The Writings of Henry David Thoreau, Vol. 5." *The Writings of Henry David Thoreau.* Houghton, Mifflin, 1898. Google Books. Web. September 2016.

Whitman, Walt. "Song of Myself, Part 24." *Leaves of Grass.* Infoplease. Web. September 2016.

Whitman, Walt. *Specimen Days.* Philadelphia: David Mackay, 1892. Bartleby. Web. September 2016.